W9-DIN-872

CONTENTS

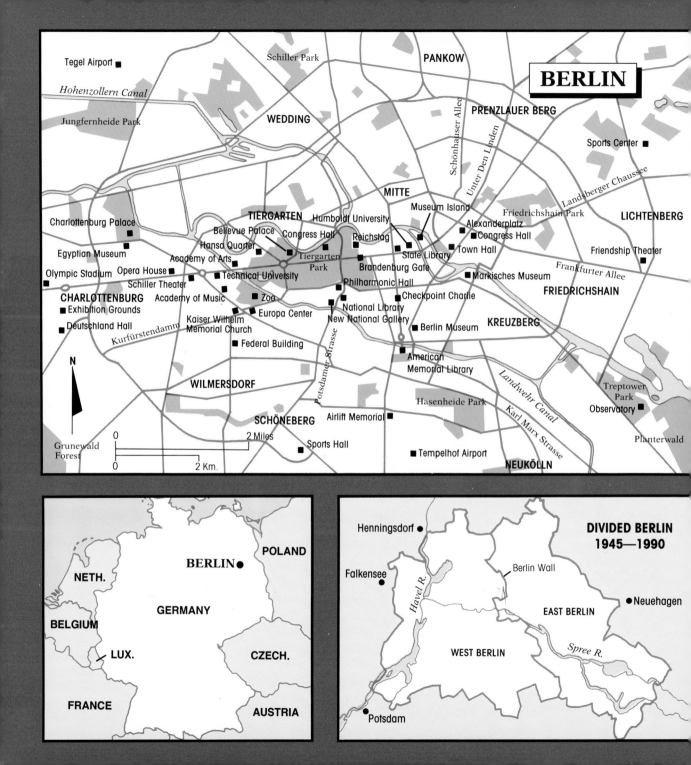

BERLIN

Tegel Airport ■

Hohenzollern Canal

Schiller Park

PANKOW

PRENZLAUER BERG

Schönhauser Allee

Sports Center ■

Landsberger Chaussee

Jungfernheide Park

WEDDING

Unter Den Linden

Friedrichshain Park

LICHTENBERG

MITTE

Museum Island

Alexanderplatz

Friendship Theater ■

Charlottenburg Palace ■

TIERGARTEN

Humboldt University

Congress Hall ■

Frankfurter Allee

Bellevue Palace

Congress Hall

Reichstag

Town Hall ■

Egyptian Museum ■

Hansa Quarter

State Library

Academy of Arts

Olympic Stadium ■

Opera House ■

Technical University

Tiergarten Park

Brandenburg Gate

Markisches Museum ■

FRIEDRICHSHAIN

Schiller Theater

Philharmonic Hall

CHARLOTTENBURG

Academy of Music

Zoo

Checkpoint Charlie

KREUZBERG

■ Exhibition Grounds

Europa Center

National Library

Berlin Museum ■

■ Deutschland Hall

Kaiser Wilhelm Memorial Church

New National Gallery

Kurfürstendamm

■ Federal Building

Potsdamer Strasse

American Memorial Library

N

WILMERSDORF

Treptower Park

Landwehr Canal

Observatory ●

Grunewald Forest

Hasenheide Park

Karl Marx Strasse

Planterwald

0   2 Miles

SCHÖNEBERG

Airlift Memorial ■

0   2 Km.

Sports Hall ●

■ Tempelhof Airport

NEUKÖLLN

NETH.

POLAND

BERLIN ●

BELGIUM

GERMANY

LUX.

CZECH.

FRANCE

AUSTRIA

Henningsdorf ●

DIVIDED BERLIN
1945—1990

Falkensee ●

Berlin Wall

Havel R.

EAST BERLIN

● Neuehagen

WEST BERLIN

Spree R.

● Potsdam

Population: 3,100,000

Size: 341 square miles (883 square kilometers)

Government: Berlin became the capital of united Germany on October 3, 1990. It had been the capital of Germany from 1871 until 1945, when Germany was defeated in World War II. Following Germany's defeat, Berlin became a divided city. West Berlin was an independent city as well as a federal state of West Germany. East Berlin was the capital of the German Democratic Republic (East Germany). Today Berlin has one mayor, and all city services—for example, police, fire protection, transportation, and hospitals—are united.

Ethnic Makeup: The population of Berlin is largely German. However, about 9 percent of the population is non-German. The largest non-German ethnic groups are Turks, Yugoslavians, Greeks, and Italians.

Religion: Most Berliners are Protestants. The next largest groups are Roman Catholics and Muslims.

City Symbol: The bear (from Berlin's old coat of arms).

Economy: High-tech electronics: chemicals; pharmaceuticals; machine building; tourism; education; the arts; civil service.

Geography: Berlin lies on a flat plain in north-central Europe. Forty percent of the city's area is covered with forests, parks, and water. The largest lake is the Grosser Müggelsee (3 square miles/7.5 square kilometers) in eastern Berlin. Berlin's two rivers are the Spree and the Havel.

Weather: Average daily temperatures in December: high 35° Fahrenheit; low 25° Fahrenheit. Average daily temperatures in July: high 75° Fahrenheit: low 55° Fahrenheit.

Highest Point in the City: TV tower at Alexanderplatz, in the eastern part of the city (1,197 feet/ 365 meters).

THE PLACE

"In a few moments the German Democratic Republic accedes to the Federal Republic of Germany. With that, we Germans achieve unity in freedom. It is an hour of great joy. It is the end of many illusions. It is a farewell without tears."
Prime Minister Lothar de Maiziére of East Germany (October 2, 1990)

"After 40 years of bitter division, Germany, our fatherland, will be reunited. This is one of the happiest moments of my life."
Chancellor Helmut Kohl of West Germany (October 2, 1990)

The Brandenburg Gate is probably Berlin's most famous landmark. This photo also shows the graffiti-scarred Berlin Wall—which was gradually dismantled in 1989–1990.

On the evening of November 9, 1989, Americans turned on their TVs and saw an astonishing scene on the nightly news. In Berlin, Germany, hundreds of people were standing on top of the Berlin Wall, the 35-mile (56-kilometer) stone barrier that had split the city in two since August 1961. With champagne bottles in hand, people hugged and kissed and danced, and some even chipped away pieces of the Wall with hammers and chisels. Earlier that day, the communist government of East Germany had decided to allow the citizens of East Berlin to travel freely to the western part of the city for the first time in 29 years.

Since 1961, the Wall had zigzagged through Berlin, cutting streets in half, dividing plazas, and separating families. In some parts of the city, it cut through abandoned lots covered with weeds. In other parts, it ran directly alongside apartment houses. On the East Berlin side of the Wall, police had forced tenants to move, and then bricked up the windows to prevent anyone from leaping to freedom in West Berlin. Sometimes they had demolished buildings entirely, creating a no-man's land laced with mines and other explosives and watched by armed guards in towers. But in one day, everything had changed. The Wall was opened, and people were joyfully dashing back and forth from one part of Berlin to the other. In just 328 days, the "City of the Wall" would become one city again.

Arriving in Berlin

Visitors approaching Berlin by airplane from any-where in western Europe will see below them a huge city. From the air, there is no sign that a wall had divided Berlin for 29 years and created, in fact, two Berlins. The total area of the capital of Germany is 341 square miles (883 square kilometers), but the city and its suburbs are twice as large, extending 28 miles (40 kilometers) from east to west.

From the window of the plane you see that much of Berlin is covered with trees and lakes. In the western half of the city alone are 50 square miles (130 square kilometers) of forests and parks. As you get closer to the ground, you notice that Berlin has no skyscrapers. One of the tallest buildings in the city—the Europa-Center—is only 22 stories high.

The trip from Tegel Airport to the center of Berlin is brief. The 20-minute ride takes you through what appears to be a modern and prosperous city. The streets and neighborhoods have the same names they had before the war, but almost all the buildings have been rebuilt since 1945. Berlin's great stone build-ings and historic monuments were pounded to rubble by American and British bombs in the final years of World War II.

You have arrived in the part of the city that used to be called "West Berlin." Although Berlin legally became one city in October 1990, the visitor will notice a distinct difference between the western and

A view of the main terminal and parking lot of Tegel Airport. Almost all travelers arriving by air from the west land at Tegel, Berlin's busiest airport.

eastern parts of the city. West Berlin is modern, with new buildings, luxurious hotels and restaurants, and streets filled with well-dressed people. The eastern part of Berlin—"East Berlin," the former capital of communist East Germany—is less modern in appearance, and its people seem poorer when compared to West Berliners.

These differences are likely to disappear over the years, but they are still visible today, even after the unification of Germany and its capital city. This chapter will first describe the western part of Berlin and then move east to look at the part of the city that was blocked off by the Wall for more than 29 years.

West Berlin

West Berlin is a city of neighborhoods, each with its own character, appearance, and mix of cultures.

Traveling around West Berlin is relatively easy; it has one of the best public transportation systems in the world. There are more than 80 bus lines, 70 miles (112 kilometers) of subway (called the U-Bahn), and 3 elevated train lines (called the S-Bahn). When the Wall went up in 1961, most of the S-Bahn lines were left in East Berlin. To make up for the loss, the government of West Berlin expanded the subway system. Today it has nine lines that serve all parts of the city. When the city was unified in 1990, the subway and elevated trains in both parts of Berlin were once again united.

Berlin is served by one of the most efficient subways in the world. Like the city, the subway system was divided after the Wall went up in 1961, but it was reconnected after 1989.

As a visitor, your first stop is likely to be a hotel near the Kurfürstendamm, West Berlin's main avenue. Called "Ku'damm" for short by Berliners, it is a 2.5-mile (4-kilometer) boulevard lined with modern hotels, theaters, discos, and restaurants, and with expensive shops and department stores. This area is the busiest part of West Berlin, the part of town that never goes to sleep.

At the head of the Ku'damm stands the Kaiser Wilhelm Memorial Church, which is both a church and a monument to the bombing during the war. Only the old church's damaged bell tower remains. Berliners called it the "decayed tooth" because of its resemblance to a tooth that's lost its filling. The new part of the church—two octagonally shaped buildings with honeycomb windows—has been built around the bell tower.

A few blocks from the Memorial Church is one of Berlin's great parks and recreational areas—the 630-acre (255-hectare) Tiergarten. Local joggers and tourists from all over the world can be seen on its grounds, enjoying the many trees and varieties of plants or visiting the zoo and aquarium on its southwestern fringe. Across the street from the zoo is West Berlin's main railroad station, appropriately named the "Zoo Station."

Cutting through the center of the Tiergarten is a long avenue that ends at the most famous symbol of Berlin—the Brandenburg Gate, a 65-foot (20-meters)

The Kurfürstendamm, West Berlin's main boulevard, is home to tourists, students, punk rockers—and even an occasional organ grinder.

A monument to the past. And a building of the future? The Reichstag (parliament) building housed a museum of German history after Germany's defeat in World War II. When the government of unified Germany eventually moves to Berlin, the Reichstag is expected to become the seat of the parliament of the Federal Republic of Germany.

high stone arch built more than 200 years ago. Before 1989, a stroll through the Tiergarten toward the Brandenburg Gate would have ended abruptly at the Berlin Wall, which stood directly in front of the arch. A few steps away from the Brandenburg Gate is the Reichstag, the parliament building of prewar Germany. After being burned in a fire probably set by the Nazis in 1933, the building went unused until it was repaired after the war. On October 4, 1990, the parliament of unified Germany held its first meeting in the Reichstag building.

Although only five minutes by subway from the hectic and modern Kurfürstendamm, the area around the Brandenburg Gate and Reichstag for many years resembled a ghost town. This once-thriving center of old Berlin had become the most famous part of the Wall, visited mainly by tour buses and an occasional jogger. But late in 1989, the Wall in front of the Brandenburg Gate was opened, and life returned to this previously deserted area. Within days, the Berlin Marathon race was run from West to East Berlin, with runners by the thousands passing beneath the great stone arch.

A 10-minute subway ride from the Zoo Station takes you to a district called Kreuzberg. Less than a mile southeast of the Brandenburg Gate, Kreuzberg is a neighborhood of artists, students, punk rockers, workers, and a large number of retired people. It is also the home of about 30,000 Turkish citizens. Their customs and culture give many of Kreuzberg's streets the feel of being in Istanbul. A major neighborhood attraction every Friday night is the Turkish market that sells vegetables, fruit, and Middle Eastern food. The noisy and cramped streets of Kreuzberg are lined with working-class apartment houses, Turkish restaurants and specialty shops, and trendy art galleries. With its unique mix of people, Kreuzberg has been compared to New York's Greenwich Village.

West Berlin's middle-class residential areas are located to the south and west of Kreuzberg. The Schöneberg district was the seat of West Berlin's government. The Schöneberg Rathaus (city hall) contained the offices of the mayor and senate of West Berlin. Many Americans

The Tiergarten, one of Berlin's many parks, is small enough to be easily covered in a day by strolling one of its many footpaths.

are familiar with the Schöneberg Rathaus as the site of a speech by President John F. Kennedy in June 1963. From the balcony of the city hall, the president said, "Ich bin ein Berliner" ("I am a Berliner") to a cheering crowd of 400,000 West Berliners. After Kennedy was assassinated in November 1963, the square in front of the city hall was renamed John-F.-Kennedy-Platz. Schöneberg is one of the oldest districts of West Berlin, but its buildings and streets have a modern look. Like so many parts of the city, it was largely rebuilt after the war.

Two subway stops to the west of Schöneberg is the Wilmersdorf district. A middle-class residential area with a large elderly population, Wilmersdorf has 50 apartment houses built solely for retired people. After the Russian Revolution of 1917, some 100,000 Russians settled in Wilmersdorf. Today, the district still has a Russian Orthodox Church and a number of Russian restaurants. The most recent residents of Wilmersdorf are Turks, who practice their religion at the Wilmersdorf Islamic center.

West Berlin's wealthiest areas are on the western edges of Wilmersdorf. Neighborhoods such as Grunewald Forest, also lie to the west. This wooded area extends 12.5 square miles (32 square kilometers) and contains a mix of oak, beech, and pine trees. Deer, wild pigs, and many species of birds live on the 274 acres (111 hectares) set aside as a natural game preserve. At the northern end of the forest is the highest land point in West Berlin—the Teufels-berg (Devil's Hill), a 394-foot (120-meters) high hill created from the debris left from the bombing.

The Grunewald Forest lies on the east bank of the Havel River, which runs through the extreme western part of West Berlin. Near the Grunewald Forest the Havel widens to form many lakes and inlets, including West Berlin's largest lake, the Grosser Wannsee. Southwest of the forest is the Wannsee Beach, where thousands of Berliners come to swim, sail, and hike during the summer months. Easily reached from downtown West Berlin by bus, the Wannsee area is one of the largest lakeside resorts in all of Europe. In the years when the Wall cut West Berlin off from the surrounding countryside, recreational areas like Grunewald and Wannsee were the only places people could escape from the city to relax.

Other large areas of West Berlin are also set aside as forests. In the northwest are the Spandau and Tegel forest, and in the extreme northern part of the city is the old village of Lübars, which is preserved as a historic site. Lübars is surrounded by fields and meadows and is the site of West Berlin's last farm-lands.

A journey of five miles directly to the south of Lübars would return you to the center of the Tiergar-ten. En route, you would pass through two residential neighborhoods with very different atmospheres.

The Tegel Palace, built in the sixteenth century, was later used by the Great Elector as a hunting lodge. In the northern part of Berlin, the palace is situated in a landscaped park first laid out in 1792 and later redesigned by the early nineteenth-century architect Karl Friedrich Schinkel.

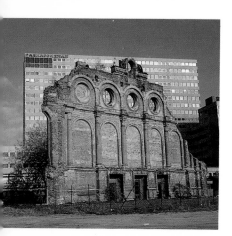

Although most of Berlin was rebuilt after World War II, a few startling ruins still remain. Above are the shattered remains of the Anhalter railroad station, near Potsdam Square.

Reinickendorf, the site of the Tegel Airport, has woods and lakes in its northern sections but is also the site of a huge "satellite town," a planned village called the Brandenburg Quarter. The 690-acre (280-hectare) project is home to some 50,000 West Berliners. With an area larger than the Tiergarten, the Brandenburg Quarter is an example of the kind of mass-produced housing built in the 1960s.

The adjoining district of Wedding is the most densely populated part of West Berlin, an area of working-class apartment houses and a sizable Turkish population. Before the war this neighborhood was known as "Red Wedding" because its population was largely sympathetic to the Communist Party. Today, the district is not so obviously working class, although many people work in Wedding's computer and electrical industries.

West Berlin is a unique mix of contrasts—Germans living side by side with Turks; modern buildings alongside historically preserved landmarks; and lakes and forests near densely packed working-class neighborhoods.

But there is another Berlin—to the east.

East Berlin

Walking on the streets of East Berlin is a journey through a city caught between the past and the future. Even the most casual visitor would be able to see the difference in appearance between this part of

Unter den Linden is the main boulevard of East Berlin. During the period when that part of Berlin was the capital of communist East Germany, Unter den Linden became a strange mix of modern, Soviet-style buildings alongside carefully preserved historic buildings. At the end of this wide street is the Brandenburg Gate.

the city and West Berlin. After the war, East Berlin was not rebuilt as quickly or as thoroughly as was the western part of the city. When it was, reconstruction often followed the style of East Germany's ally, the Soviet Union. Buildings were torn down to make way for wider avenues and immense plazas. New buildings, constructed in the 1950s and 1960s, tended to be large and box-like and did not in any way resemble the look of prewar Berlin. War-damaged ruins were often left untouched for years; even today, bullet-scarred buildings can be found all over the neighborhoods of East Berlin.

If you walk through the Brandenburg Gate, you will be on a street called Unter den Linden, the mile-

A statue of King Frederick II of Prussia (1740–86) on Unter den Linden in Berlin. During his reign, many new buildings and parks were created throughout the city.

long main avenue of East Berlin. At the heart of the Mitte district of East Berlin, Unter den Linden (which means "Under the linden trees") is a wide, tree-lined street that is a mix of the new and the old.

Near the Gate sit many foreign embassies and government offices, all built in the drab style of the 1950s. Farther down the street are a number of great historic stone buildings that date from the 1700s and 1800s. All were destroyed or damaged in the bombing but have been restored to their original appearance. Among them are the National Library, the campus of Humboldt University, and the Opera House. The extreme end of Unter den Linden is the site of some of the finest museums in Europe: the Pergamon, the Altes Museum (Old Museum), the National Gallery, and the Bode Museum.

These carefully restored buildings contrast sharply with the flat emptiness of the Marx-Engels-Platz, which is directly across the Spree River from the museums. Before the war, this square was known as the Lustgarten, the site of an old botanical garden and the royal palace. Rather than restore the site to its original appearance, the communist government in the 1950s leveled it and created the current square, which was used for large party rallies. The square is flanked by two huge Soviet-style buildings built in the 1970s: the Foreign Ministry and the Palace of the Republic.

The Friendship Fountain at Alexanderplatz, a modern square built during the communist period in East Berlin.

A block away is Alexanderplatz, the heart of East Berlin and the most modern square in this part of the city. Rebuilt in 1968, Alexanderplatz is a vast space reserved for pedestrians and surrounded by modern buildings. Traffic is routed through tunnels below the square, which is also the site of the tall TV tower so easily spotted from anywhere in the city.

A visit to these public areas of East Berlin will show another contrast with life in West Berlin. The pace of life in East Berlin is much slower. There are fewer pedestrians and less traffic. By contrast with the western part of the city, these vast public squares seem almost empty.

But there are other parts of East Berlin that reveal its special quality. Near Alexanderplatz is the district of Prenzlauer Berg, which is the most heavily populated area of East Berlin. Here you find cafes and bars and an atmosphere somewhat like that of Kreuzberg district of West Berlin but without the diverse ethnic mix found in the west.

The housing in other residential areas of East Berlin contrasts sharply with buildings in West Berlin. In the east, people live in older buildings that are often in great need of repair. Some parts of East Berlin were less heavily bombed than neighborhoods

A statue of Lenin, the founder of the Soviet state, in front of the old Soviet embassy in East Berlin. This embassy, which was located on Unter den Linden , was closed down along with other foreign embassies when East Germany and West Germany united in 1990.

in the west, and homes and apartment houses often date from before the war.

Like West Berlin, the eastern part of the city has an extensive network of parks and forests. In the extreme southeastern quarter of East Berlin is the Köpenick Forest, the site of the city's largest lake, the 3-square-mile (7.5 square kilometer) Müggelsee. The surrounding forest is hilly and has nature trails and cafés where hikers can rest. The wooded area near the Müggelsee is East Berlin's equivalent of the Grunewald Forest in the west.

Berlin Today

The opening of the Berlin Wall brought a quick change in the pace of life in both Berlins. Suddenly, people who had lived side by side but separately for 29 years were able to freely explore each other's part of the city. For East Berliners, it was an opportunity to shop in the well-stocked stores in the west and to bring home bananas and other fresh fruits that were impossible to get in the east. For West Berliners, it was an opportunity to buy goods at lower prices in the east and to visit the many historic landmarks and museums of Berlin that were east of the Wall.

With unification, the main boulevards and wide plazas of the east now have more visitors from the west. And the normally bustling streets of West Berlin are even more jammed as the "eastern cousins" discover what life in the west is like.

THE
PAST

Berlin will always be Berlin.
—Old German Saying

The corner of Unter den Linden and Friedrich Strasse in the heart of Berlin at the beginning of the twentieth century. Although the old German saying is that "Berlin will always be Berlin," this part of the city was completely destroyed in World War II and has since been rebuilt.

BERLIN. Unter den Linden
Friedrichstraßen-Ecke.

Charlottenburg Palace was built beginning in 1695 as a country house for the wife of Elector Frederick III. It is now a museum that sits in the center of a large, landscaped park.

The city that is today Berlin was first settled in the 1200s. Two villages—one called Berlin and the other called Kölln—were founded on the Spree River. Historical records from the period first mention Kölln as a town in 1237, and the first reference to a "Berlin" appears in 1244. At that time, the land was covered with sand and thick forests. The early settlers lived a hard life raising cattle and trying to grow crops in the poor soil.

There was no central government in Germany at this time, and settlements were protected by knights who built castles and other fortifications to guard the towns and villages. The Spree River was shallow between Berlin and Kölln and easy to cross. The towns were a natural meeting place for cattle herders and traders, and by the end of the 1200s they had become centers of trade and commerce. In 1307, they merged and built a common town hall.

Early History

During these years, roving bands of robbers and knights attacked cities and villages all over the region, and town dwellers were forced to form their own militias. When a prince of the Hohenzollern family of Nürnberg gained control over the surrounding region of Brandenburg in the early 1400s, peace returned to Berlin. In 1406, Berlin became the principal city and meeting place of the Electors (or Princes) of Brandenburg.

By the 1500s, Berlin's population had grown to about 12,000 as people migrated to the city from all over Germany. The economy continued to grow, and schools and churches were built. Although some Berliners became wealthy, most lived in poor conditions. There were no sewers or running water, and garbage was allowed to rot in the streets.

Under such conditions, epidemics were common. In 1576, the Plague swept through Berlin and killed almost 5,000 people. Shortly after the Plague, Berlin was reduced to poverty by the Thirty Years' War, a huge and destructive conflict that was fought all over Europe between 1618 and 1648. Although the city itself was not attacked during the war, its economy suffered, and living conditions deteriorated. By the end of the war, only 6,000 people were living in Berlin, and the city had lost the vitality it once enjoyed as a population and trading center.

Berlin was not attacked during the Thirty Years' War, which raged across Europe between 1618 and 1648, but the city was badly damaged economically.

The Great Elector

Despite the Plague and the hardships of the Thirty Years' War, Berlin soon recovered. The great Hohenzollern ruler Elector Frederick William (1640–1688), who is known as "the Great Elector," did much to revive the city. He encouraged free trade and the construction of new buildings and canals. Between 1662 and 1668, the Oder-Spree Canal was built. This new waterway, which linked the North Sea with Breslau to the east, made Berlin an important port.

In the late 1600s, there was much religious persecution throughout Europe. The Great Elector, an enlightened ruler, allowed more than 5,000 French Protestants, who were known as Huguenots, to settle in Berlin after being expelled from France in 1685. Some of these people brought with them wealth and business skills that contributed to the rebuilding of the city. In the years that followed, Berlin became known as a place of refuge for those fleeing religious persecution as well as for those interested in becoming wealthy through trade and commerce.

As Berlin recovered, the Hohenzollern rulers consolidated their power and extended their rule into regions east of Berlin. In 1657, the Great Elector obtained control over a territory called Prussia from the king of Poland. In 1701, Frederick William's son and successor, Elector Frederick III, had himself crowned "king of Prussia" and was known from then on as King Frederick I. With his coronation, the Kingdom of Prussia was born, with Berlin as its chief city.

Frederick the Great

One of the greatest periods in Berlin's history occurred under King Frederick II (1740–1786), who is known as "Frederick the Great." During his reign, the center of Berlin was redesigned and new buildings and parks were created. Working with King

Frederick, the architect Georg Wenzeslaus von Knobelsdorff built the Rheinsberg Palace and a new opera house. He also laid out a number of new parks in Berlin and at Frederick's palace, Sans Souci, located southwest of the city in Potsdam. Throughout Berlin, new drainage projects, roads, and canals were constructed. In 1750, cotton and silk factories were built, and Berlin became the largest textile-producing city in Germany.

Frederick the Great, like the Great Elector, was a supporter of art and science. A composer himself, he enjoyed the company of philosophers, artists, and musicians. While he was king, the greatest minds of Europe gathered in Berlin and at Frederick's palace in Potsdam.

Although his reign brought growth and prosperity to Berlin, Frederick was never popular with the people. As a military and political leader, the king led Prussia into many conflicts. Some of these wars reached the gates of Berlin. The city was occupied briefly by the Austrians in 1757, during the Seven Years' War, and in 1760 by Russian troops. Nevertheless, by the end of Frederick's reign, Prussia was a great power that was deeply involved in European military and political affairs.

King Frederick II of Prussia (Frederick the Great) made his country a major European power. In the process, Berlin became a center of learning and the arts.

Berlin in the Early 1800s

By 1800, the population of Berlin was 200,000. As the capital of Prussia, it had a prosperous middle class of businessmen and merchants who had very little political power. The Prussian kings were all-powerful and had little desire to share their power with other groups in society.

The challenge to their rule came from outside Prussia's borders. In 1789, three years after Frederick the Great's death, the king of France was overthrown in the French Revolution. In a few short years, a previously unknown soldier named Napoleon Bonaparte gained power and began a campaign of military conquest throughout Europe.

In 1806, Napoleon's forces defeated the Prussian army at the Battle of Jena and a short time later marched into Berlin. For the next three years, the city was occupied by French troops.

French rule stirred feelings of German nationalism. But it also brought to Berlin many of the ideals of the French Revolution—especially political liberty and freedom. Napoleon's victories had weakened the Prussian kings, but after Napoleon was defeated in 1815, the monarchy regained its power and authority. A popular saying of the time was that when Berliners were denied political freedoms, they "retreated to their pleasures." This period, during the long reign of Frederick William III (1797–1840), saw the appearance of Berlin's first bars and cafes. Instead of politics, business and money-making became more important. The search for a more democratic society would wait until another time.

The Revolution of 1848

That time came in 1848, a year of unrest through-out Europe. In Vienna and Paris, revolutions by the poor and middle classes broke out against kings. The uprising soon spread to Berlin, which became the center of the revolution in Prussia against King Frederick William IV. Hundreds died in the fighting in the streets of Berlin. For a time, the revolutionar-ies seemed to have won, and the king was forced to grant a new constitution. But by the end of 1848, the forces loyal to the monarchy regained control of Berlin, and the revolution was crushed.

The Revolution of 1848 swept over Europe and brought death and destruction to Berlin. In the end, the revolutionaries were defeated and the monarchy remained in control of the state.

Otto von Bismarck is considered the founder of the German Empire. Under his iron-willed leadership, Prussia became the leading force in unifying Germany in the 1870s.

With political reforms once again defeated, Berlin began a new period of economic growth and change. Between 1850 and 1900, the city became the second largest industrial center of Europe. Large corporations set up factories that manufactured heavy machinery, and people from all over Germany moved to Berlin in search of work. But many found only slums and poor living conditions, and as much as half of the city's population was poor.

With the rapid growth of the working class, Berlin became the center of the trade union movement and of other groups calling for social justice, the elimination of poverty, and political democracy. The political arm of these groups was the Social Democratic Party, which was to play an important role in German politics in later years.

By 1866, Prussia controlled much of what was to become modern Germany. In that year, Berlin became the capital of the North German Confederation, a loose political union of many German states dominated by Prussia. The North Germany Confederation was the first step toward the unification of Germany under the Prussian monarchy. In 1870, Prussia went to war against France and won. Strengthened by their military victory, the Prussians, led by their "Iron Chancellor," Otto von Bismarck, declared the creation of the "Second German Empire" in January 1871. The new German emperor, William I (1871–1888), was crowned at Versailles.

Imperial City

The defeated French were required to make payments of money to their German conquerors, and much of this money was used to further develop the economy of Berlin. As new industries were built, the city spread out into its surrounding suburbs. Slum housing continued to be built within the city, but more workers were now living outside of Berlin. In 1879, the first electric lights were installed in the city, and two years later, the first telephones went into operation. Public transportation in the early days of the empire consisted of horse-drawn carriages and railroads that connected the city with surrounding areas. But by 1900, more and more automobiles and buses came into use, and in 1902, Berlin's first subway line began operating.

The first 30 years of the German Empire were a period of dynamic growth for Berlin. The city's population, which was around 900,000 in 1871, grew to more than 2.5 million by 1900. Berlin soon gained a reputation as a center of free thinking and modern trends. In all areas—art, science, business— imperial Berlin was the major city in Germany and even all of Europe.

Berliners may have encouraged new and different thinking, but the German government was still run by an emperor who respected and encouraged the Prussian military tradition. William II (1888–1918) hated his capital city. While on a visit to Norway in

Traffic in Berlin became more congested and dangerous in 1905, when the first motor buses began to operate in the city.

1892 he wrote: "There is nothing in Berlin that can captivate the foreigner except a few museums, castles, and soldiers. . . . The Berliner does not see these things, and would be very upset were he told about them."

But the emperor, not the citizens of Berlin, ran the government, and it was this very government that led Germany into World War I in 1914. The German people at first supported the war. In fact, crowds gathered in Berlin in August 1914 screaming, "We want war! We want war!" But the conflict that everyone thought would be over in a few months lasted four years and caused great hardship. In Berlin, prices skyrocketed and food and coal ran out. By 1918, many people had turned against the war and began pressuring the government to get out of the conflict. Berlin, as a large city with a huge population of poor and middle-class people, became a center of opposition to the war and to the monarchy. With Germany near defeat, Emperor William II abdicated in November, 1918 and fled to Holland.

The Weimar Period

With Germany's surrender in 1918, Berlin entered a period of great instability. Street violence, strikes, and rebellions in the ranks of the military were common throughout the city. Fearing total loss of control, the conservative government that survived the Emperor's abdication surrendered power to the

Social Democratic Party. It was their unhappy task to try to create a democratic government.

In the winter of 1918–1919, Berlin was a city in turmoil. Workers' militias marched through the streets alongside rebellious soldiers and sailors. In early 1919, the communist Spartacus party called a general strike and set up barricades under the Brandenburg Gate. Government troops were called in and the uprising was crushed.

To escape the disorder and danger in Berlin, delegates who were elected to form the new German government retreated to the small city of Weimar, southwest of Berlin. There they created Germany's first democratic government, which became known unofficially as the "Weimar Republic."

Another uprising shook Berlin in 1920, when right-wing military groups attempted to overthrow the new government. They were defeated after trade unions and the government called for a strike.

Although street violence eventually ended, the Weimar Republic remained politically unstable. Germany had no tradition of democratic government. As in the 1800s, there were too many groups clashing with each other and preventing democracy from taking root. But it was during this period—the 1920s—that Berlin became the leading cultural capital of the world. Europe's largest filmmaking studio, UFA, was located at Babelsberg, a few miles from Berlin. Movie stars like Greta Garbo and

World War I caused great shortages of food and coal for citizens of Germany. By 1918, the people of Berlin—who had cheered for war years earlier—were protesting for its end.

The great international movie star Marlene Dietrich began her career in Berlin during the 1920s, when the city was one of the major cultural centers of the world.

Marlene Dietrich and the director Fritz Lang started their careers in Berlin. In other areas—music, theater, and art—Berlin became the leading city of Europe.

In 1920, most of the surrounding suburbs were incorporated into Berlin, a change that increased the city's size more than 10 times. By the mid-1920s, more than 4.5 million people lived in greater Berlin. Industry moved into the suburbs, and more and more people moved from the city to surrounding communities.

But with the coming of the world economic collapse called the Great Depression, German politics entered a new period of instability. As economic conditions worsened in the early 1930s, millions of people lost their jobs. Democratic government was again under attack, this time from the Nazi Party led by Adolf Hitler.

The Nazis were never popular among the tolerant Berliners, who regarded them as gangsters from southern Germany. In 1929, the Nazis moved in force into Berlin in order to provoke street fights with their opponents. Berlin voters responded by giving the Communist Party a majority in the national election of 1930.

Berlin Under the Nazis

But Hitler was not to be stopped, and the Nazis soon came to power. On the day Hitler became

Chancellor of Germany—January 30, 1933—Nazi supporters staged a huge torchlight parade under the Brandenburg Gate. Berlin was entering the darkest period of its history.

The Nazis brutally suppressed all opposition. Political opponents were arrested or murdered and the press was censored. In May 1933, a huge book burning, designed to destroy the works of "un-German" authors, was carried out at Humboldt University. Hitler and thousands of Nazis presided over the famous summer Olympics, held in Berlin in 1936. It was there that black American runner Jesse Owens ruined Hitler's intended demonstration of Aryan supremacy by winning four gold medals. In November 1938, synagogues and Jewish-owned businesses in Berlin were burned on what became known as *"Kristallnacht"* (Crystal Night), named after the shattered glass that littered the streets the morning after the attack. During the 1920s, some 160,000 Jews lived in Berlin. By 1939, about 58,000 had been able to flee Germany. Except for a handful, the remaining 100,000 died in Nazi concentration camps.

In September 1939, Germany invaded Poland, and within days the country was at war with Great Britain and France. This time, no one ran through the streets crying "We want war!" Berliners remembered the hardships of World War I and were fearful about what was to come. In 1941, the Soviet Union

Adolph Hitler, Nazi leader and dictator of Germany from 1933 until 1945.

A Nazi "storm trooper" boycotting a Jewish-owned shop in Berlin in 1933. Almost all of Berlin's Jewish citizens were either forced to flee Germany or were killed in concentration camps.

The Brandenburg Gate as it appeared on May 8, 1945. The wreckage around the arch remained from the battle for Berlin, during which the Soviet army stormed the city.

and the United States joined in the war against Germany. The conflict that followed—World War II—lasted until 1945. When it was over, Berlin lay in ruins. At the start of the war the head of the Nazi air force, Hermann Goering, said: "If one bomb falls on Berlin, you can call me a Dutchman." By 1943, Berliners were calling him "the fat Dutchman," as American and British planes flew over the city day and night dropping thousands of tons of bombs.

These great raids, which reached their peak between 1943 and 1945, destroyed most of Berlin and killed more than 70,000 people. Over 1 million people fled the city, and another 100,000 died when the Soviet army attacked Berlin in April 1945.

In May 1945, after the surrender of Germany, Berlin was no longer a city, but a vast area of bombed-out buildings. There was no gas, electricity, or running water. Buses, subways, and elevated trains had stopped running. Factories, office buildings, and apartment houses had been turned into piles of shattered bricks. People wandered through the streets bewildered and dazed, and rats and bugs swarmed over the devastated city. The survivors were mostly women, children, and old people who lived in wrecked buildings and basements.

Berlin after World War II

Immediately following the defeat of Germany, Berlin was placed under the rule of the Allied nations

During the Soviet blockade of Berlin in 1948–1949, the United States and its allies flew food and other supplies into the isolated city. Planes were forced to fly a dangerous path into Tempelhof Airport, which was situated in the middle of the city and surrounded by buildings.

that had won the war—the United States, Great Britain, France, and the Soviet Union. Although Berliners soon took control over many local government responsibilities such as police, sanitation, and firefighting, the real power over the city rested with the four victors of World War II.

But Berlin was 110 miles (177 kilometers) inside the Soviet occupation zone of Germany, and the presence of American, British, and French forces in the western and southern parts of the city irritated the Soviets. Thus, Berlin became a center of the rivalry between the United States and the Soviet Union known as the Cold War.

In 1948, Stalin, the Soviet dictator, decided to test the will of the United States to remain in Berlin. In June of that year, he cut off West Berlin from the rest of Europe by blockading all roads and canals into the surrounded city. Stalin hoped to isolate West Berlin and drive out the American, British, and French. Because it was surrounded on all sides, West Berlin depended for its survival on food and other products brought in from the outside.

The Berlin Wall began in 1961 as a barbed-wire fence. Over the years it became a heavily fortified stone barrier protected by guards and mine fields. This picture shows the Wall being strengthened in 1966.

Denied access by land, the United States and its allies organized a huge airlift of food, coal, and other vital materials. For 10 months, hundreds of flights a day flew from West Germany into Berlin's Tempelhof Airport, bringing in more than 2 million tons of goods. Despite the bad weather in the winter, the flights continued to come. Eventually, the Soviet Union gave in and ended the blockade in May 1949. West Berlin had survived the greatest threat to its existence since World War II.

In October 1949, the Soviet section of Berlin officially became the capital of East Germany, a communist country created out of the Soviet occupied zone in Germany. A year later, in October 1950, the American, British, and French occupation zones joined together with their own constitution. Berlin was now officially two cities.

Despite this political division, Berlin functioned as one city. People moved freely back and forth between East and West Berlin. Some people even held jobs in one section and lived in the other. Berlin's subways, elevated trains, and telephone system continued to operate in both parts of the city as if there were no division.

West Berlin became more and more prosperous in the years after the war. Large portions of the city that were destroyed in the air raids were gradually rebuilt. People began to enjoy a higher standard of living as the city recovered from the war.

The existence of a free and thriving West Berlin was a great embarrassment to the communist government of East Germany. Between 1950 and 1960, more than 100,000 people left East Germany for the west. Most of them did so simply by traveling on the elevated train or subway from East Berlin to West Berlin.

In order to stop this enormous population drain, the East German government began building a wall down the center of Berlin in August, 1961. Over the years, the Berlin Wall was expanded and strengthened. Even though it stood 16 feet (4.5 meters) high and was 8 feet (2.4 meters) deep in some parts of the city, people still tried to escape from East Berlin. Dozens were shot trying to jump to freedom in the west.

With the building of the Wall, travel between the two parts of the city was severely restricted. If you lived in West Berlin, or if you were a foreigner, you would have to go to one of several checkpoints to get into East Berlin. The most famous was "Checkpoint Charlie," which was guarded on the western side of the Wall by American troops. At any checkpoint, you would be forced to pay an entry fee to get into East Berlin, and you would often wait hours before the guards would let you through. In the 1970s and 1980s, the East Germans eased travel restrictions somewhat, but traveling between West and East Berlin was never without some difficulty.

"Checkpoint Charlie" was one of the few openings in the Wall through which visitors were allowed to enter East Berlin.

The End of the Wall

Early in 1989, thousands of East Germans discovered a new way to flee to West Germany—by traveling first to the neighboring countries of Hungary, Czechoslovakia, and Poland, and from there to the west. With living conditions worsening and political freedoms still denied them, some 200,000 East Germans abandoned their country in 1989.

Hoping to stop the loss of more of its people, the communist government in East Germany took a risk and decided to allow East Germans to travel freely to West Berlin and West Germany. Within hours, thousands of people were moving freely between East and West Berlin. At first, the Wall had a few new checkpoints opened to handle the increased traffic between the two parts of the city. But soon entire sections were torn down.

A few weeks later, communist authority in East Germany collapsed altogether. On March 18, 1990, the first free elections in 57 years were held in East Germany. The population voted overwhelmingly to unite with West Germany.

In July 1990, the economies of West Germany and East Germany were united, with the West German *Deutschemark* becoming the currency in East Germany. Political union came on October 3, 1990.

In slightly less than 11 months, the city that many felt would be divided forever by the huge stone wall down its center was united again.

One City. One Nation. Berlin: October 3, 1990.

The change came suddenly. But when it came, it unleashed other changes that could not be reversed. On the night of November 9, 1989, Berliners from both sides of the city danced on top of the Wall near the Brandenburg Gate. Few would have guessed that on another cool autumn evening—just 10 months and 24 days later—more than a million Germans would gather around the Brandenburg Gate to celebrate the unification of East and West Germany and of the city of Berlin.

The Wall near the Gate—that familiar yet unnatural monument to hatred and division—was now almost completely gone. Where it had once slashed in front of the Brandenburg Gate stood throngs of jubilant Berliners. All through the evening the crowds grew. At midnight on Wednesday, October 3, 1990, West Germany and East Germany became one country. At the same time, Berlin became one city. Fireworks exploded over the Brandenburg Gate, and the million people gathered near the historic arch erupted in loud cheers.

Chancellor Helmut Kohl (center) at a ceremony attended by East German and West German officials. Lothar de Maiziére (second from left), was the last prime minister of East Germany before unification.

What actually happened at the moment of unification? Richard von Weiszäcker, president of West Germany, became president of united Germany. Helmut Kohl, chancellor of West Germany, became chancellor of united Germany.

At that moment, 144 members of the former East German government joined the 519 members of the West German parliament to become the parliament of united Germany.

Lothar de Maiziére, the last prime minister of East Germany, became a member of the new cabinet of united Germany, along with three other officials of the former East German government.

And, in one instant, the 1.9 million citizens of West Berlin and the 1.2 million people of East Berlin were joined to become residents of the largest city on the European continent between Paris and Moscow.

THE PEOPLE

All free men, wherever they may live, are citizens of Berlin. And therefore, as a free man, I take pride in the words "Ich bin ein Berliner". ("I am a Berliner").

**President John F. Kennedy
Speech in West Berlin,
June 26, 1963**

Café life has always been an important part of Berlin's culture. On a warm and sunny day, people gather on the Kurfürstendamm to sip coffee and to people-watch.

When John F. Kennedy told the cheering crowd at the Schöneberg Rathaus that "I am a Berliner," he was expressing a feeling that millions of people—both Germans and non-Germans—have had over the years.

Before Berlin was founded, the surrounding region was populated by a Slavic-speaking people called the Wends. They were pagans, and they lived in small villages and farmed the sandy soil of the region. In the 1200s, descendants from the original Germanic tribes began moving into the area from the western part of Europe. These new settlers were Christians, and they soon conquered the Wends. It was under the Germans that Berlin began to develop as a town.

Berliners of the Past

The earliest non-German Berliners were the 5,000 French Protestant Huguenots who moved there in 1685 to escape from religious persecution in their homeland. They were eventually allowed to build their own churches and schools, and they contributed to the economic and cultural development of the city. In the 1700s, other refugees—Swiss and Austrian Protestants and Jews from all over Europe—came to Berlin in search of religious freedom. The city soon gained a reputation as a refuge, a place where people could start over—a place with a future.

The reign of the Great Elector (1640–1688) and his successors produced some of the most notable artists

The playwright Bertolt Brecht wrote the librettos for two of Kurt Weill's operas, including The Three-penny Opera. Weill's wife, the singer Lotte Lenya, pictured here with Brecht, played the leading roles in many of Weill's works.

and architects in Berlin's history. Andreas Schlüter (1660–1714) was an architect and a sculptor. His statue of the Great Elector can still be seen in the courtyard of the Charlottenburg Palace. Frederick the Great, who reigned from 1740 to 1786, had as his court architect Georg Wenzeslaus von Knobelsdorff (1699–1753), who built several palaces as well as the opera house that still stands in East Berlin.

Immigrants continued to flock to the city in the 1800s, but they began to come now from areas east of Berlin—from Poland, East Prussia, and Silesia (a region in Eastern Europe now divided between Poland and Czechoslovakia). Unlike the Protestants and Jews from western Europe, these new immigrants were poor. Once in Berlin, they became workers in the city's growing industries, and they lived in the slum housing that was built for the thousands of new arrivals.

By the 1920s, Berlin was the cultural capital of Europe. The population was overwhelmingly German, but the city had also become home to artists, writers, and entertainers from all over the world. Notable Berliners of this period included the great theatrical producer Max Reinhardt, who founded the Deutsches Theater, and the world-famous playwright Bertolt Brecht, whose works dealt with social struggle and the conditions of the poor. The composer Kurt Weill rose to fame in Berlin in the 1920s. His most famous work, *The Three-penny Opera,*

The German-born composer Kurt Weill began his career in Berlin during the 1920s but later moved to the United States, where he composed musicals and wrote occasionally for the movies.

which he wrote with Brecht, is forever identified with Berlin culture in the twenties.

World War II brought another wave of migration to Berlin. As Germany started to lose the war, a wave of refugees from the east, fleeing the Soviet army, crowded into the city. Despite the bombing, these people hoped that they would be safe in the German capital. After the defeat of Germany in 1945, millions of ethnic Germans were expelled from East Prussia and Poland, and many ended up in Berlin. Even though the bombing had left vast portions of the city in ruins, people stayed there, hoping that times would eventually get better.

In the first bleak years after the war, one Berliner rose to prominence as a political leader. Ernst Reuter (1889–1953) had left his native city in 1933, after Hitler came to power. Returning to Berlin in 1947, he was elected mayor in 1948 but was prevented from taking office by the Soviets, who had veto power over his election. Reuter rallied the people of Berlin during the Soviet blockade and eventually became mayor in 1950.

Berlin's most famous postwar politician was Willy Brandt, who was elected mayor of West Berlin in 1957 and was still in office at the time the Wall was built. He later went on to become chancellor of West Germany (1969–1974). In 1971, Brandt was awarded the Nobel Peace Prize for his efforts to promote world peace.

Max Reinhardt founded the Deutsches Theater. He was one of Germany's greatest theatrical producers in the 1920s.

Over the centuries, many different peoples had come to Berlin in search of freedom and a chance to better their lives. Berliners took pride in their spirit of tolerance toward outsiders, a sentiment that Frederick the Great expressed when he said, "Everyone shall be happy here in his own fashion."

Berliners Today

It would be difficult to describe "typical" Berliners today. They are the Turks and punk rockers of Kreuzberg as well as the wealthy residents of Grunewald. They are also the workers of Wedding and the elderly people of Wilmersdorf. And they are the citizens of East Berlin who lived on the other side of the Wall.

Only a little more than half of the current residents of West Berlin were born there. Even many of the citizens of East Berlin were not born in the city but instead moved there from other parts of East Germany. Berliners like to say, "If you like Berlin and decide to stay, you are a Berliner."

The truth of this saying has been challenged in recent years as more non-Germans and people with diverse lifestyles have settled in West Berlin. When the Wall was built in 1961, East Germans who had worked in West Berlin were suddenly cut off from their jobs. Overnight, West Berlin needed thousands of new workers. The shortage of skilled workers was made worse by the fact that many young people

Mayor Willy Brandt of West Berlin (left) escorting President John F. Kennedy on a tour of the city during the president's 1963 visit to Berlin.

chose not to stay in the surrounded city but instead moved to West Germany, where they had a greater choice of jobs and more freedom of movement.

In response to the labor shortage, the West German government invited foreigners—who were called "guest workers"—to move to West Berlin. In the 1960s, thousands of men from Turkey, Yugoslavia, Greece, and other countries of southeastern Europe came to West Berlin and took jobs. Most left their families back in their homelands and intended to stay in Berlin only for a year or two in order to earn money before returning home.

However, many remained in the city and eventually brought their families to West Berlin. Today, some 260,000 non-Germans live in West Berlin. The largest group by far are the 120,000 Turks. From the "Little Istanbul" section of Kreuzberg to the Turkish areas of Wedding, their influence can be seen all over the city.

Life has not been easy for the Turks of West Berlin. They tend to have low-paying jobs and live in the poorer sections of the city. The first generation of "guest workers" now have children who were born in West Berlin and are caught between two cultures. On the one hand are their Turkish-born parents, many of whom maintain strict Muslim traditions and wish their children to marry only Turks. On the other is the German society that does not fully accept them because of their different culture.

The Turks of Berlin have preserved many aspects of their culture, despite the difficulties of living in a foreign country. Their neighborhood in the Kreuzberg section of the city is often called "Little Istanbul."

Despite these and other difficulties, the Turks of Berlin have maintained their cultural traditions. They have their own newspapers, a TV station, and a wide variety of groups designed to help Turks in the city. Throughout West Berlin are more than 25 mosques where the Turks can practice their Islamic faith. Most of these mosques are not new buildings but instead have been established in old factories that are no longer in use.

Berliners, like most Germans, enjoy the tradition of afternoon coffee and cake at a local *Konditorei*—in English, a "sweet shop."

The Turkish influence is seen all over the streets of West Berlin, even outside Kreuzberg. While walking down the Kurfürstendamm, for example, a visitor will come upon food stands that offer the traditional German sausage with a Turkish twist: a side of curry ketchup or mustard as a topping. Turkish restaurants are found throughout the city, and Turkish people work in all kinds of businesses.

As more and more young people left West Berlin after the Wall was built in 1961, the average age of the remaining population became older. The elderly of West Berlin were almost all ethnic Germans and almost all were residents of Berlin before the war. These survivors of the war can still be seen in the city, whether in the residential neighborhoods of Schöneberg and Wilmersdorf or in Kreuzberg. East Berlin also has a large population of elderly people, also mainly prewar residents who survived the war and chose to remain in their native city.

The elderly of Berlin are what Germans call *Rentners:* people on government pensions. Taking care of their needs—social security payments, hospital and nursing care, and subsidies for rent—takes up a large share of the city budget. As a group, the war survivors are becoming fewer as each year passes. A person who was 30 years old when the war ended would now be 75, and as this generation dies, an important living connection with a bygone era slowly disappears.

Although many young people left Berlin in the 1960s, others from West Germany were attracted to the city. With the Wall cutting the city so completely in two, West Berlin soon got a reputation as a "free city," a city caught between the East and the West and belonging to no one.

The new breed of young people were rebels; they were not interested in the "establishment" or in the middle-class values. As more and more of them moved to Berlin, they began to form communities, especially in Kreuzberg and Wedding. In 1968, they organized anti-war demonstrations against the conflict in Vietnam. In the 1970s, some of them became involved in the struggle to ban nuclear weapons, while others grew interested in the environmental movement.

The "new" young people were highly visible and were often noisy. To the traditional middle-class of Berlin, they seemed to dress strangely and were involved in unpleasant and disruptive political demonstrations.

By the 1980s, these young people—who were part of what Berliners called "The Scene"—were in open conflict with the city government and the business community. Many of them had become "squatters"—that is, they took over abandoned buildings, especially in Kreuzberg, and restored them to their original appearance. When many of the original owners of these buildings attempted to have the

Many of the young people of Berlin were swept up in the anti-war sentiments of the 1960s. Like the young of other countries, they held street demonstrations to protest the American war in Vietnam.

squatters evicted, the senate of West Berlin attempted to resolve the conflict. A law was passed allowing the squatters to remain in their buildings if they could show that they were hoping to preserve them. The government of West Berlin realized that the young people had in fact improved many buildings that had been left to decay. In some cases, they had even added solar energy, thus helping lessen the city's traditional reliance on coal as a source of energy for heating.

By 1990, there was less tension between the young and the city government. The young people continued to live in their communities, where they ran their own self-help groups, restored and improved old buildings, and advocated causes aimed at improving the environment. In some ways, they had become an accepted part of life in West Berlin.

For 29 years, the people of West Berlin—the elderly and the rebellious young, ethnic Germans and ethnic Turks—had lived side by side with Berliners on the other side of the Wall. They had very little contact with each other during these years. When they did, it was only on rare occasions allowed by the East German government and only for short periods. It was as if a close member of your family lived in a room in your house in which you were not allowed to enter. Then one day, the door was opened. The incredible scene that Americans saw on their TVs on the night of November 9, 1989, marked the first day that the people of East and West Berlin had the freedom to get to know each other once again.

The streets of West Berlin—especially the Kurfürstendamm—were filled with the new visitors from the East. They were easy to spot. They came in small, old cars that belched gasoline fumes and contrasted sharply with the big, shiny West German Mercedes and BMWs. Their clothes often set them apart, too—they were plain and sometimes even a bit shabby. They lined up at the banks of West Berlin to collect the small "allowance" of $67 that the West German government promised to each man, woman, and child who came over from East Germany. But mostly, they simply stood in front of store windows filled with clothing, stereos, VCRs, and all the other symbols of prosperity in West Berlin. They stood and just stared, sometimes with a look of amazement on their faces. They did not have such things in East Berlin.

The majority of East Berliners went back through the Wall that evening of November 9. They now had the freedom to come back any time they wished. There would be time for that—time to acquaint themselves with a part of their city that had been off limits to them for almost 30 years. But that night, they slept knowing that their city was divided no more.

ON THE TOUR BUS

Any visitor touring this huge city will quickly see that Berlin is a unique combination of the old and the new. It is impossible to see all of Berlin on foot, but you may choose to travel around the city on the U-Bahn or S-Bahn, or you may take a Berolina Bus tour that begins on the Kurfürstendamm and visits the major points of interest throughout the city.

Landmarks

Brandenburg Gate. More than any other landmark, this 65-foot (20-meter) high stone arch is the symbol of Berlin; located at the end of Unter den Linden (East Berlin).

Kaiser Wilhelm Memorial Church, at the beginning of the Kurfürstendamm (West Berlin). Built between 1891 and 1895, the church was almost completely destroyed by the bombing in 1943. Today, a modern, octagonal-shaped church and tower with honeycomb windows have been built around the remains of the old bell tower. Inside the church is a cross made from the

Platz der Akademie (Academy Square), a short walk from Unter den Linden, is the location of a theater (left) and the French Cathedral (right).

nails found in the wreckage of Coventry Cathedral in England, which was destroyed during the war by German bombers.

Reichstag (parliament building), a few steps north of the Brandenburg Gate (West Berlin). Built in the late nineteenth century, it was the home of the old German parliament and of the first meeting of the united

German parliament in 1990. Its exterior still has bullet marks from the war, but its west wing has been restored and houses a museum of German political history.

Olympic Stadium, in Charlottenburg (West Berlin), near the Havel River. Built by the Nazis for the 1936 Olympics, it holds 100,000 spectators. Although still in use, it is remembered as a symbol of the Nazi era.

TV Tower, at Alexanderplatz (East Berlin). It was built in 1969 and at 1,197 feet (365 meters) is the second highest structure in Europe. An observation platform and a revolving restaurant are located about 610 feet (186 meters) above street level.

St. Hedwig's Cathedral, on Französischer Strasse (East Berlin). Erected in 1747, it was the first Roman Catholic church to be built in Berlin after the Protestant Reformation. A circular building, it is similar to the Pantheon in Rome.

Marienkirche, on Karl-Liebknecht Strasse (East Berlin). Built in the thirteenth century, this church was restored in 1950.

Nicholas Quarter, across the street from the Marienkirche. This is a restored area of medieval buildings and cobblestone streets. Many of the old homes were restored using photographs and paintings. This unique section of East Berlin was opened to visitors in 1987, the 750th anniversary of the founding of Berlin. The area takes its name from the Nicholas Church, built in the twelfth century and the oldest church in Berlin.

Museums

Some of the finest museums in Europe are found in Berlin.

Museum Island, in the Spree River (East Berlin). This is the site of three of Berlin's finest museums. *The Pergamon Museum* is famous for its exhibits of ancient art and architecture. The most prominent—from which the museum takes its name—is the Pergamon Altar, a Greek temple found in Turkey and built in 180 B.C. Museum Island is also the

The TV Tower in East Berlin dominates the skyline of the city.

The Kaiser Wilhelm Memorial Church is framed by a sculpture on the Tauentzien Strasse.

location of the *National Gallery,* with its collection of nineteenth- and twentieth-century paintings and sculpture, and the *Bode Museum,* which has pieces dating from as far back as the Egyptian and early Christian periods.

The Dahlem Museum, Arnimallee and Lansstrasse (West Berlin), is housed in one building but has seven sections: a painting gallery, a gallery of sculpture, museums of Indian art, Islamic art, and East Asian art, a museum of ethnography, and a collection of prints and engravings. The Dahlem Museum will soon move to new quarters in the Tiergarten section of the city.

Palaces

A number of Berlin's most famous museums are located in historic palaces that have been restored to their original appearance.

Charlottenburg Palace, on Spandauerdamm (West Berlin), was begun in 1695 as a country house for the wife of Elector Frederick III. It was expanded over the years and is now a museum. The exterior of this long and narrow building is painted yellow and is topped by a dome 157 feet (47 meters) high. Among Charlottenburg's exhibits are the historical apartments,

The Airlift Memorial near Tempelhof Airport was built in 1951 to commemorate the 1948–1949 airlift that kept Berlin alive during the Soviet blockade.

some of which look as they did during the time of Frederick the Great. The palace is in the middle of a great courtyard and park. At the west end of the park is a mausoleum that contains the graves of the Emperor William I and his wife, Empress Augusta Victoria.

The Bellevue Palace, located in the Tiergarten (West Berlin), was built in 1785 as a summer residence. Destroyed in the war, it was completely rebuilt and now serves as one of the official residences of the president of West Germany. The palace's park contains trees that were donated by the British people after the war.

Köpenick Palace, Schlossinsel (East Berlin), is the location of the Museum of Applied Art, with its collection of pottery, porcelain, and furniture. The surrounding park is home to many kinds of rare birds.

Parks and Lakes

Berlin is a "green" city. More than 40 percent of its total area is taken up by trees and water. The *Grunewald Forest* in West Berlin is 12.5 square miles (32 square kilometers) in area and contains a mix of oak, beech, and pine trees. It is the site of a nature preserve and a historic hunting lodge. In the center of downtown West Berlin is the *Tiergarten*, a 630-acre (255-hectare) park that

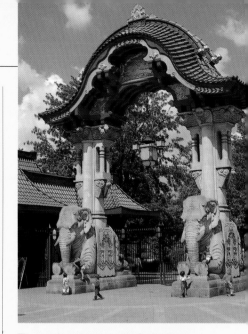

The ornate entrance to the Berlin Zoo, which is located on the southwestern edge of the Tiergarten.

contains many species of trees and flowers. At its southwestern edge is the *Berlin Zoo*, which has almost 11,000 animals and birds. Berlin's largest lake is the *Müggelsee* (3 square miles/7.5 square kilometers), in East Berlin. It stands in the middle of the *Köpenick Forest*, a vast area of hilly woods and streams that occupies the southeastern section of East Berlin. The Köpenick Forest is the East Berliner's equivalent of the Grunewald.

Universities

Although Berlin has many schools, three stand out as the most important.

Humboldt University, on Unter den Linden (East Berlin) is the oldest university in Berlin. Founded in 1810 and originally called Frederick William University, it has been the home to some of the world's greatest scholars, including Albert Einstein, the founder of nuclear physics. The *University of Technology* in Charlottenburg (West Berlin) was founded in 1879 and is the second oldest university in the city. When Berlin was divided, Humboldt University was left in the Soviet zone. In order to have a university in the west, the *Free University of Berlin* was founded in 1948. Situated in the Dahlem section of the city, it has 50,000 students and is the largest university in West Berlin.

Cultural Events

There is no shortage of cultural events to attract the visitor to any part of Berlin. No matter what time of year, the city is the site of many festivals and exhibitions.

The Berlin International Film Festival has been held every year in West Berlin since 1951. In addition, an *international art festival*, also founded in 1951, is held every autumn with displays from artists all over the world.

Berlin is a city of music. West Berlin is the home of the *Berlin Philharmonic*, one of the world's greatest symphony orchestras.

East and West Berlin each has a major opera company. The *German Opera—Berlin* performs in West Berlin in a building constructed in 1961. The *German National Opera*, in East Berlin, is located at the restored Opera House on Unter den Linden. For those who enjoy more modern music, a festival called *Berlin Jazz Days* is held every autumn in West Berlin.

West Berlin has three state theaters and smaller companies scattered throughout all parts of the city. East Berlin is the home of the *Berlin Ensemble*, which was founded by the famous playwright Bertolt Brecht in 1949.

West Berlin is host to a number of annual folk festivals. The *Franco-German Folk Festival* and the *German-American Folk Festival* are held each summer to celebrate German, French, and American culture. Tourists who enjoy browsing will come upon many open-air markets throughout Berlin. The weekly Turkish market in Kreuzberg specializes in Middle Eastern food and other products. The city's largest outdoor market is held every Wednesday in the square in front of Schöneberg Rathaus, West Berlin's city hall. The city also has many smaller flea markets that sell goods ranging from clothing to household appliances to foreign foods.

The opera house (right), home of the German National Opera, is located on Unter den Linden.

1244	First reference to a "Berlin" in historical records.
1576	Berlin devastated by the Plague.
1618–48	Thirty Years' War. Berlin's population declines to 6,000 people.
1640–88	Reign of the Great Elector, Frederick William; growth of Berlin as a major city.
1685	5,000 French Huguenots settle in Berlin.
1701	Berlin becomes the capital of Prussia.
1740–86	Reign of Frederick the Great; Berlin becomes a major city of Europe.
1806–09	Berlin occupied by French troops.
1848	Revolution of 1848. Hundreds killed in Berlin before revolution is crushed.
1871	Berlin becomes the capital of the German Empire.
1879	First electric lights in Berlin.
1881	First telephone service in Berlin.
1902	First subway opens in Berlin.
1914–18	World War I.
1919	Berlin becomes capital of the Weimar Republic.
1920	Berlin absorbs surrounding suburbs and increases 10 times in land area.
1933	Adolph Hitler becomes leader of Germany.
1936	Summer Olympics held in Berlin.
1939–45	World War II. Much of Berlin destroyed by American and British bombers.
1945	Berlin occupied by the victorious Allies following Germany's defeat.
1948–49	Blockade of West Berlin by the Soviets.
1949	East Berlin becomes the capital of East Germany.
1950	American, British, and French zones of Berlin officially become the city of West Berlin.
1961	East Germany starts building the Berlin Wall.
1989	Berlin Wall is opened as East Germany allows its citizens to travel to the West.
1990	First free elections in East Germany in 57 years. East and West Germany united (October 3). Berlin united and becomes the capital of Germany.

For Further Reading

Finke, Blythe F. *Berlin: Divided City* (Topics of Our Times Series, No. 1). D. Steve Rahmas, ed. SamHar Press, 1973.

Francisco, Ronald, and Richard L. Merritt. *Berlin Between Two Worlds.* Westview, 1988.

Shirer, William L. *Berlin Diary: The Journal of a Foreign Correspondent, 1939–1941.* Little, 1988.

Steins, Richard. "Berlin," in *The New Columbia Encyclopedia,* pp. 279–280. Columbia University Press, 1975; and "Brandenburg," in *The New Columbia Encyclopedia,* pp. 356–357. Columbia University Press, 1975.

Tusa, Ann, and John Tusa. *Berlin Airlift.* Atheneum, 1988.

Where to Get More Information

For brochures and lists of cultural events, you may write to the *Berlin Tourist Information Office* (Berliner Verkehrsamt), Europa-Center, Budapesterstrasse, D-1000 Berlin 30, Germany.

In the United States, information on Berlin may be obtained at the *German National Tourist Office,* 747 Third Avenue, New York, 10017.

INDEX

Photo credits

Cover, page 20, 57 (left), 58 (right), Steve Vidler/Leo de Wys Inc.; p. 4–5, 11, 14, 19, 56, Fridmar Damm/Leo de Wys, Inc.; p. 8–9, 13, 59, J. Messerschmidt/Leo de Wys, Inc.; p. 12, 17, 31, 34, 37 (bottom), 38, 39, 43, 49, 51, German Information Center; p. 15, 58 (left), Adrian Baker/Leo de Wys, Inc.; p. 18, 52, Danilo Boschung/Leo de Wys, Inc.; p. 21, J. Kappelmeyer, Leo de Wys, Inc.; p. 22, 44–45, Charles Graham/Leo de Wys, Inc.; p. 24–25, Max A. Polster Archive; p. 26, 57 (right), German National Tourist Office, New York; p. 35, 37 (top), 48, The Bettmann Archive; p. 36, Springer/Bettmann Film Archive; p. 40, 53, UPI/Bettmann Newsphotos; p. 41, Reuters/Bettmann; p. 46, 47, Kurt Weill Foundation.